Keep Quilting

with Alex Anderson

- 7 Skill-Building Piecing Techniques
- 16 Traditional Blocks to Mix & Match
- 6 Sampler Star Projects

C&T PUBLISHING

DEDICATION

This book is dedicated to my friends.

My life has been blessed with a multitude of wonderful people whom I treasure deeply. Each shares a unique "life spirit" that continues to profoundly affect and enrich my life. I am very grateful to have this diverse community of friends who understand me and love me just for me.

Five very special women—Cheryl, Dee, Elizabeth, LeAnna, and Paula— lent their talents to make this book a reality. I am sure you will agree that they are phenomenal quilters. They are also truly amazing friends.

Text © 2005 Alex Anderson
Artwork © 2005 C&T Publishing

PUBLISHER: *Amy Marson*

EDITORIAL DIRECTOR: *Gailen Runge*

ACQUISITIONS EDITOR: *Jan Grigsby*

EDITOR: *Liz Aneloski*

TECHNICAL EDITORS: *Joyce Engels Lytle and Teresa Stroin*

COPYEDITOR/PROOFREADER: *Wordfirm*

COVER DESIGNER: *Christina D. Jarumay*

DESIGN DIRECTOR/BOOK DESIGNER: *Rose Sheifer*

ILLUSTRATOR: *Richard Sheppard*

PRODUCTION ASSISTANT: *Kerry Graham*

QUILT PHOTOGRAPHY: *Sharon Risedorph*

Published by C&T Publishing, Inc.,
P.O. Box 1456, Lafayette, CA 94549

Library of Congress Cataloging-in-Publication Data

Anderson, Alex,
  Keep quilting with Alex Anderson: 7 skill-building piecing techniques, 16 traditional blocks to mix & match, 6 sampler star projects.
    p. cm.
  ISBN 1-57120-280-3 (paper trade)
1. Patchwork--Patterns. 2. Quilting--Patterns. I. Title.
TT835.A49367 2005
746.46--dc22
2004027243

Printed in China

10 9 8 7 6 5 4 3 2

CONTENTS

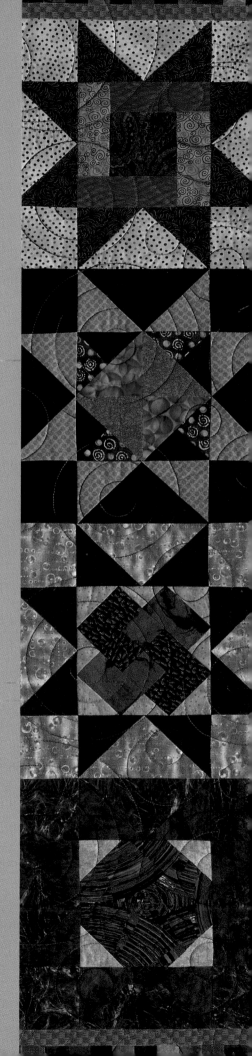

INTRODUCTION

I am very excited about the publication of this book, and especially about the fact that you are picking it up to take a peek! This tells me that you have probably already made a quilt and want to continue learning more about this fabulous craft.

The sky is the limit in quilting, so let's take the next step together, developing new skills by working with stars. I love star blocks, and the Sawtooth Star may well be my all-time favorite. I also love sampler quilts (quilts made from many different blocks), and I believe that Sawtooth Star blocks that incorporate various smaller blocks—or "bellies"—are the perfect way to accomplish this goal.

By making your quilt with the blocks in this book, you will learn many different techniques that will serve you well in your quiltmaking journey for years to come. Together, we'll explore seven different piecing techniques. At a minimum, I suggest that you make a Sawtooth Star that includes a block from each category.

I am lucky to have many quilting friends in my life. I called upon five of my friends to make quilts using the blocks in this book. We started with a sewing day at my house and then parted ways, excited and energized by each other's choices of fabrics. When the quilts were gathered weeks later, the results were astonishing! Each quilter's personality sang through her work. Let me introduce you to these fabulous women:

LeAnna Christopher (*Autumn,* page 24) is a delightful young lady who came into my life a few years ago. You may be familiar with her work from my book *Kids Start Quilting* or as the superb teenage guest on my television program, *Simply Quilts.* Although LeAnna hasn't made dozens of quilts (yet!), she has certainly been bitten by the bug and especially excels with her machine quilting. Both her mom and I are envious of her innate talent. It would be safe to say that LeAnna has taken to quilting like a duck to water. She has her mom, Dee Christopher, to thank for their shared quilting passion.

In addition to being LeAnna's mom, Dee Christopher (*Basket Bouquet,* page 28) is an assistant, supportive ally, and friend to me. She has been quilting for several years and has introduced many adults and children to the wonderful world of quilting. Her gentle spirit and artistic eye make even the most basic quiltmaking classes an experience in creativity and confidence-building for new quilters. That gentle spirit is beautifully reflected in the quilt she made for this book. If you are lucky, you might have the pleasure of bumping into both Dee and Elizabeth Scott at the quilt shop in my California hometown.

Elizabeth Scott (*Check and Balance,* page 40) is a talented quilter whose background stems from interior design. In addition to "growing" her pattern company, Late Bloomer Quilts, Elizabeth makes the time to share her talents with me. We have had the pleasure of creating and working together on several projects. This book began with an idea Elizabeth suggested during one of our many brainstorming sessions. I find her thought process very similar to mine, yet uniquely her own. Not only is her work stunning to the eye, but it also has a quality of workmanship I greatly admire.

I first met my wonderful friend and neighbor Cheryl Uribe (*Crop Circles,* page 36) when she was a student in one of my classes. Her career as a hairdresser was stopped short due to an allergic reaction to hair dye. Shortly thereafter, she acquired a longarm machine and has since been discovering the joy of longarm quilting. Cheryl has immersed herself in all aspects of quilting, and the time spent has paid off well. Her hip, young-at-heart approach to all aspects of design is evident in her sampler.

My pleasure in working with Paula Reid (*It's Harvest Time,* page 32) has been long-standing. She is an expert machine quilter and has gotten me out of a pinch—I hate to admit!—on more than one occasion. Many of the machine-quilted quilts I own were enhanced by her masterful work. Paula recently moved to a house with a Tuscan feel and the influence shows beautifully in this quilt, which features several hand-dyed fabrics.

I can't begin to describe my response to the quilts as I viewed them in their finished state. I was overwhelmed by the result of my friends' work. I even got goose bumps! I am pleased to share their quilts with you. In addition to her quilt, I asked each quilter for a tip she found useful in the quilt's construction. These tips are listed within the instructions for each quilt.

So … it's time to get started! As you make your quilt, feel free to experiment with the countless possibilities for block and fabric choices and for layout. The quilts in this book only begin to explore the possibilities. Remember that when you work in a sampler format, the quilt often takes on a personality of its own. Your job as quiltmaker is to "listen" to the quilt and be willing to take some unexpected turns. For me, this is one of the best parts of quiltmaking. Enjoy the process, and I hope we meet one day soon!

"MAGIC" CUTTING NUMBERS

The instructions for each method of making the Sawtooth Star tell you how large to cut the pieces for the 12" and 6" Star blocks featured in this book. The instructions for each pieced center block include the necessary cutting information as well. All of the instructions include "magic" cutting numbers for easy and accurate rotary cutting.

Suppose you'd like to change the size of the finished block? How do you know how—and how large—to cut the pieces? Just use the magic cutting numbers!

There are two basic rules for using the magic numbers.

- The magic cutting numbers work only when you are using a standard ¼" seam allowance.

- Add the magic cutting number to the *finished* size of the desired piece. Do not consider the ¼" seam allowance; the magic number does that for you.

It's so easy! The magic numbers remain constant no matter what size block you are making. See the block diagrams on page 13 to identify pieces A–D.

SQUARES

Use this magic number to cut the four corner squares (C) for the Sawtooth Star, regardless of the method you are using to piece the block. If you plan to make the star center (D) a single piece rather than a pieced block, use the same magic number. In fact, you can use this magic number to determine the cut size of any finished square piece in this book.

Cut a square the finished size of the desired piece *plus* ½" in both directions.

Magic Number
Finished size + ½"

TRIANGLES

Before you apply the magic number for cutting triangles, you must determine if you need a half-square triangle or a quarter-square triangle. The difference is determined by where you want the straight of grain to fall. It is typically on the outside edge of the pieced unit or block; otherwise, your block can easily become stretched and distorted.

On the half-square triangle, the straight of grain falls on the two short sides adjacent to the 90° angle. On the quarter-square triangle, the straight of grain falls on the long side opposite the 90° angle.

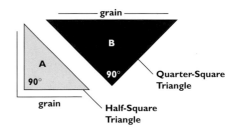

The Sawtooth Star block includes both types of triangle: the half-square triangle for the star points (A) and the quarter-square triangle for the star background (B).

Half-Square Triangle

Use this magic number for Method 1: Cutting Triangles (page 13) and Method 3: Secret Sawtooth Star (page 14) (A) or to determine the cut size of any half-square triangle in this book.

Cut a square the finished size of the piece *plus* 7⁄8" in both directions. For Method 1, cut the square in half diagonally. For Method 3, use the square as is.

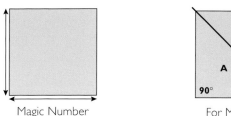

Magic Number
Finished size + 7⁄8"   For Method 1

Quarter-Square Triangle

Use this magic number for Method 1: Cutting Triangles (page 13) and Method 3: Secret Sawtooth Star (page 14) (B) or to determine the cut size of any quarter-square triangle in this book.

Cut a square the finished size of the piece *plus* 1¼" in both directions. For Method 1, cut the square in half diagonally in both directions. For Method 3, use the square as is.

Magic Number
Finished size + 1¼"   For Method 1

SQUARES AND RECTANGLES FOR SEW AND FLIP (Method 2)

For Method 2: Sew and Flip (page 14), you will cut the star points (A) as squares and the star backgrounds (B) as rectangles. The triangles magically appear when the pieces are sewn, trimmed, and pressed.

Cut 2 squares the finished size of the short side of the unit plus ½" for A.

Cut a rectangle the finished size of the unit *plus* ½" in both directions for B.

Finished size of unit

Magic Number
Finished size + ½"

GENERAL INSTRUCTIONS

FABRIC

Fabric is the "soul" of the quilt. I recommend you use 100% cotton fabric, in the very best quality you can find, for your quilts. Believe me, you'll be pleased with the results: good quality cotton handles well for accurate cutting and piecing, turns under nicely for appliqué, and stands up well to laundering and use.

I prewash the fabric I put into my quilts, and here's why. Cotton can shrink when washed for the first time, so prewashing eliminates the potential for puckers and distortion in your finished quilt. It can also remove excess dye or alert you to unstable color that can bleed or run when you wash your quilt later. Finally, prewashing removes any chemical residue introduced in the manufacturing process.

CHOOSING FABRICS

Each of the project quilts includes a feature titled Dynamite Design Options, which provides a brief discussion of the fabrics each quilter selected, how she used them as a springboard for the quilt design or quilting motif, and suggestions for alternative fabric choices. In addition, the following is some general information on making fabric choices for your quilts.

Choosing fabric is probably one of the biggest—and often most challenging—decisions we quiltmakers must make. For many people, it is a paralyzing experience. I prefer to look at it as an opportunity to learn and to grow in my quiltmaking!

Decide on the theme or look of your quilt. My rule of thumb is: the more different fabrics you can incorporate into your quilt, the more exciting it will be. Periodically visit your local quilt shop to see what's new, and add to your collection regularly. Focus particularly on areas—colors or styles of prints—where your stash may be lacking. If you don't have it, you won't use it!

A focus fabric makes a great place to start in choosing the colors and prints for your quilt. Focus fabrics are those glorious fabrics that feature large-scale prints with many colors. You can often find unusual color combinations in these special fabrics, inspiring a dynamite palette for your quilt that you might not have considered otherwise. Once you've chosen your focus fabric, hunt for supporting fabrics that pick up the colors in the focus piece.

THREAD, PINS, AND OTHER GOODIES

Use a quality cotton thread. Neutral gray or tan works great for piecing.

Don't be tempted to skimp on pins. Invest in extra-fine (1⅜" or .50mm) glass-head pins. I love them for machine piecing. They may cost a bit more at the outset, but they are worth it because of the successful results. Trust me on this: using inferior-quality, bargain-brand pins will only cause you headaches!

Keep a tape measure handy to measure your quilt top for borders. A metal one works best, since fabric tapes can stretch and become inaccurate over time.

I can't imagine cutting the many pieces and strips for my quilts, as well as the borders and bindings, without my trusty rotary cutter! The medium-size cutter can cut up to four layers of 100% cotton at once, while the larger cutter cuts through six layers easily and quickly. If you're purchasing a rotary cutter for the first time, and your budget allows, treat yourself to the larger size. Otherwise, the medium one will do fine.

Choose a 6" x 24" Omnigrid or Olfa ruler, particularly for borders. Both are marked horizontally and vertically in ⅛" increments, and they identify the 45° angle that we quilters so often use. As a companion, select a self-healing mat designed specifically for use with a rotary cutter. Although you can make do with a smaller size, the larger varieties (e.g., 24" x 36") are great for cutting large border strips. An accurately marked grid also helps.

You probably already own an iron suitable for quiltmaking, but eventually you'll want to invest in a super-hot steam iron. Successful pressing is an important step in creating a well-crafted quilt.

Finally, be sure your sewing machine is in good working condition, with proper tension, an even stitch, and a sharp size 80 needle.

PINNING

Careful pinning helps you match intersecting seams easily and accurately, coax two rows of blocks together, or ease a finicky border to fit. It keeps raw edges from drifting apart as you stitch, which is a real plus when sewing long seams to add borders or bindings.

PIECING

Use a ¼" seam allowance throughout. Stitch a sample seam—or even a sample block—to make sure your seam allowance is accurate and consistent. Set the stitch length at about 12–14 stitches per inch. This is small enough to be secure, but not too tiny in case you need to use your seam ripper. If the seam will be crossed by another seam, you don't need to backstitch.

Fabric is the "soul" of the quilt.

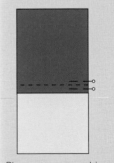

Pin seams pressed in opposite directions.　　Pin points to align exactly.

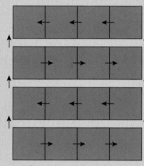

Where multiple (e.g., 6 or 8) seams meet, I often press seams open to distribute the bulk. In this case, I press *wrong* side up.

← →
press open

PRESSING

It's fairly standard practice to press seams to one side when machine piecing. I typically press them in one direction or the other based on ease of construction. The project diagrams include pressing arrows to help you.

← →
press   press

I press pieced units and blocks *right* side up on a firm surface to avoid pressing tucks in the seams. I don't press too aggressively or drag the iron across the fabric, which can distort any unstitched bias in the shapes or finished blocks.

SETTING BLOCKS TOGETHER

All the quilts in this book feature straight-set blocks (blocks that are pieced in horizontal rows). Paula's quilt *It's Harvest Time* may not appear that way at first glance, but the four center blocks are pieced in horizontal rows with sashing and then turned on point and finished with large setting triangles.

To place your blocks in a traditional straight setting, arrange the blocks side by side with the edges parallel to the quilt's edge. Sew the blocks into horizontal rows, pressing the seams in opposite directions in alternate rows. Sew the rows together, and press in one direction. I find that the seams usually tell me which way they want to go!

Please don't feel limited to the specific settings shown in the project quilts. You can arrange and rearrange these blocks—both the large Sawtooth Stars and the smaller 6" center blocks—in any number of layouts, including strippie (long vertical or horizontal rows with wide sashes in between) or diagonal sets. I hope you'll try a few of these options before making your "final" decision.

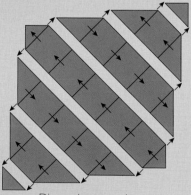

Straight set pressing

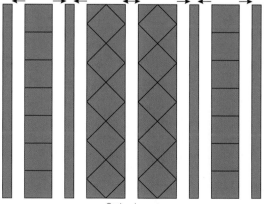

Strippie set

Diagonal set pressing

You'll probably notice that some of the 6" blocks are directional and look best when turned in a particular direction. The House block (page 18), for example, is best set vertically, with the roof up! Keep this in mind when arranging the blocks in the project quilts or when designing your own unique quilt setting.

BACKING

All the projects in this book are wider than the standard 42"-wide cotton fabric, so you'll need to piece the backing. Yardages given include at least 2" extra all around the outside of the quilt top to allow for any shifting that might occur as you quilt. (The same is true for the batting.) You'll trim the excess when you've finished quilting.

For your pieced backing, consider using your favorite fabric from the quilt top, a "what-was-I-thinking" fabric in a color that relates to the quilt top, or a variety of fabrics. Avoid dark fabrics if your quilt top is mostly light, because the dark backing can shadow through and dull the quilt.

Prewash the backing fabric and remove the selvages before seaming the pieces together. Run the seams horizontally or vertically, whichever makes best use of the fabric.

LAYERING AND BASTING

Spread the backing wrong side up on your (nonloop) carpet or work surface. Smooth the backing, and secure it with T-pins or masking tape. Center the batting on top of the backing, and trim the two layers so the raw edges match. Center the quilt top right side up onto the batting, smoothing carefully to remove any wrinkles.

For hand quilting, use large hand stitches to baste the three layers together in a 4"-grid pattern. For machine quilting, secure the three layers every 3" with rust-proof #1-size safety pins. Distribute the pins evenly, avoiding areas where you know you'll be stitching. In either case, baste all the way to the edges of the quilt top.

QUILTING

I love to hand quilt, but unfortunately I don't always have time. Instead, I determine how the quilt will be used and then decide how to handle the quilting. Whether you hand or machine quilt, I have three thoughts to share:

- When it comes to quilting, more is better. Never skimp on the amount of quilting on your quilt.

- Treat the surface as a whole. I often quilt my quilts with interesting grids that unify the design. However, I rarely quilt ¼" from the seamlines, because doing so accentuates what to me is the most unsightly part of the quilt—the seams.

- Use an equal amount of quilting over the entire surface. If you quilt different areas with unequal density, not only will your quilt look odd, but it will also sag and not lie flat.

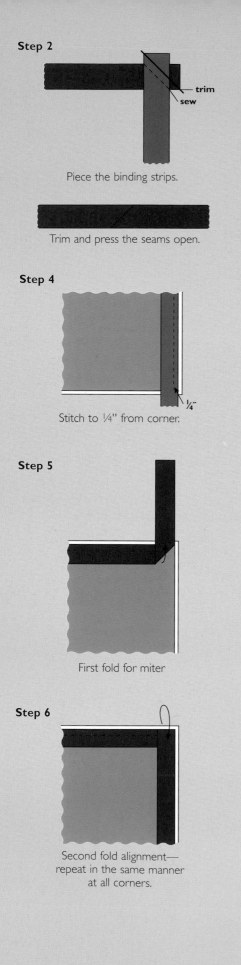

Step 2

Piece the binding strips.

Trim and press the seams open.

Step 4

Stitch to ¼" from corner.

Step 5

First fold for miter

Step 6

Second fold alignment—
repeat in the same manner
at all corners.

BINDING

1. Trim the batting and backing ⅛" beyond the raw edge of the quilt top.

2. Cut 2⅛"-wide strips from the fabric width, as directed in the project instructions. You will need to piece the strips together to get the desired length. Sew the strips together end to end with a diagonal seam. Then press the seams open. This helps prevent a big lump in the binding.

3. Fold and press the binding lengthwise, wrong sides together.

4. With raw edges even, pin the binding to the edge of the quilt a few inches from the corner, leaving the first few inches of the binding unattached. Start sewing, using a ¼" seam allowance. Stop ¼" from the first corner, and backstitch 1 stitch. For pucker-free bindings, use a walking foot attachment (or an even-feed feature, if your sewing machine has one). Adjust the needle position to achieve the desired seam allowance.

5. Lift the presser foot and needle. Rotate the quilt one-quarter turn. Fold the binding at a right angle so it extends straight above the quilt.

6. Bring the binding strip down even with the edge of the quilt. Begin sewing at the folded edge. Stop ¼" from the next corner, and backstitch 1 stitch. Repeat in the same manner at all corners.

7. Join the ends of the binding together by folding the ending binding tail back on itself where it meets the beginning binding tail. From the fold, measure and mark the cut width of your binding strip. Cut the ending binding tail to this measurement. For example, if your binding is cut 2⅛" wide, measure 2⅛" from the fold on the ending binding tail and cut the binding tail to this length.

   Open both tails. Place one tail on top of the other at right angles, right sides together. Mark a diagonal line and stitch on the line. Trim the seam to ¼". Press open.

8. Turn the folded edge of the binding over the edge of the quilt, and slipstitch the binding to the backing and form miters at the corners.

Step 7

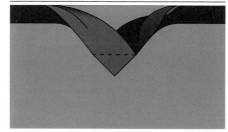

Sew ends of binding together diagonally.

BLOCK INSTRUCTIONS

Each project quilt includes a number of large (12") Sawtooth Star blocks, each featuring a smaller (6") block as its center square. I've divided the smaller center blocks into seven categories, with each category designed to introduce you to a specific piecing technique or to help you sharpen your existing piecing skills.

Clever Elizabeth Scott included a smaller, 6" version of the Sawtooth Star block in the setting for her quilt *Check and Balance* (page 40). Cheryl Uribe used this smaller block for the center in one of the large stars in *Crop Circles* (page 36), as did I in *Tutti Fruiti* (page 44), an idea you might like to try as well. Here are instructions for piecing these fabulous stars.

The following pages include all you need to know for making the 12" and 6" Sawtooth Star blocks, as well as the variety of 6" blocks. We'll start with the Sawtooth Star—our "star" of the show!

12" AND 6" SAWTOOTH STAR BLOCKS: THREE EASY METHODS

Finished block sizes: 12" × 12" and 6" × 6"

I love the Sawtooth Star block. Here are three different ways to piece it. All three methods include rotary cutting, and are fast, fun, and easy. Why not try all three and pick your favorite?

The center of the 12" block features one of the pieced 6" blocks, and the center of the 6" Sawtooth Star block is a plain fabric square (D).

Method 1: Cutting Triangles
Magic cutting numbers (page 7)

CUTTING FOR 12" BLOCK

Fabric 1
• Cut 4 squares 3⅞" x 3⅞", then cut in half diagonally for the star points (A).

Fabric 2
• Cut 1 square 7¼" x 7¼", then cut in half diagonally in both directions for the background triangles (B).
• Cut 4 squares 3½" x 3½" for the background squares (C).

CUTTING FOR 6" BLOCK

Fabric 1
• Cut 4 squares 2⅜" x 2⅜", then cut in half diagonally for the star points (A).
• Cut 1 square 3½" x 3½" for the star center (D).

Fabric 2
• Cut 1 square 4¼" x 4¼", then cut in half diagonally in both directions for the background triangles (B).
• Cut 4 squares 2" x 2" for the background squares (C).

BLOCK ASSEMBLY

1. Sew an A triangle to a short side of each B triangle. The ^ indicates which edge or point to line up. Press.

2. Repeat on the other short side of each B triangle. The ^ indicates which edge or point to line up. Press. Make 4.

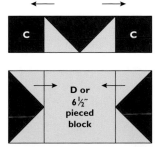

3. Lay out the pieces as shown. Sew the pieces into rows. Press.

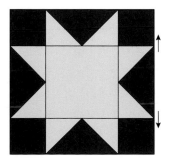

4. Sew the rows together. Press.

Method 2: Sew and Flip
Magic cutting numbers (page 7)

CUTTING FOR 12" BLOCK

Fabric 1
- Cut 8 squares 3½" x 3½" for the star points (A).

Fabric 2
- Cut 4 rectangles 3½" x 6½" for the background triangles (B).
- Cut 4 squares 3½" x 3½" for the background squares (C).

CUTTING FOR 6" BLOCK

Fabric 1
- Cut 8 squares 2" x 2" for the star points (A).
- Cut 1 square 3½" x 3½" for the star center (D).

Fabric 2
- Cut 4 rectangles 2" x 3½" for the background triangles (B).
- Cut 4 squares 2" x 2" for the background squares (C).

BLOCK ASSEMBLY

1. Draw a line diagonally, corner to corner, on the wrong side of each A square.
2. Align an A square with a short edge of each B rectangle, right sides together.

3. Sew directly on the drawn line and trim, leaving a ¼" seam allowance.

4. Press as indicated by the arrows. Make 4.

5. Repeat Steps 2–4 to sew an A square to the opposite side of the unit. Press. Make 4.
6. Assemble the block as described in Method 1, Steps 3 and 4.

Method 3: Secret Sawtooth Star
Magic cutting numbers (page 7)

CUTTING FOR 12" BLOCK

Fabric 1
- Cut 4 squares 3⅞" x 3⅞" for the star points (A).

Fabric 2
- Cut 1 square 7¼" x 7¼" for the background triangles (B).
- Cut 4 squares 3½" x 3½" for the background squares (C).

CUTTING FOR 6" BLOCK

Fabric 1
- Cut 4 squares 2⅜" x 2⅜" for the star points (A).
- Cut 1 square 3½" x 3½" for the star center (D).

Fabric 2
- Cut 1 square 4¼" x 4¼" for the background triangles (B).
- Cut 4 squares 2" x 2" for the background squares (C).

BLOCK ASSEMBLY

1. Draw a diagonal line, corner to corner, on the wrong side of the A squares.

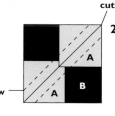

2. Align an A square with opposite corners of the B square, right sides together. The A squares will overlap in the center. Sew ¼" on each side of the drawn line. (You might find it helpful to draw the ¼" lines that you will stitch on.)

3. Cut on the drawn line between the 2 rows of stitching.

4. Press each unit open.

5. Place an A square on the corner of each unit from Step 4. Sew ¼" on each side of the drawn line.

6. Cut on the drawn line between the 2 rows of stitching.

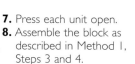

7. Press each unit open.
8. Assemble the block as described in Method 1, Steps 3 and 4.

6" BLOCK CENTERS FOR 12" SAWTOOTH STAR BLOCKS

Each of the following categories includes two blocks—except for Blocks with Diagonal Piecing (page 21), which includes a third, "bonus" selection. (It seems my quilting friends just couldn't resist the optional block I offered them!) All of the blocks finish 6" x 6".

Blocks with Strip Piecing

Some blocks include repeating units of side-by-side strips (or bars). Instead of piecing these units from individually cut pieces, you can speed up the process—and still retain accuracy—by piecing strips of the appropriate fabrics into strip sets and then cutting the strip sets into the number of segments you need for the block (or blocks).

 ### Monkey Wrench Block
Finished block size: 6" x 6"

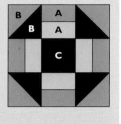

CUTTING

Fabric 1
• Cut 1 strip 1½" x 13" for the Monkey Wrench bars (A).

Fabric 2
• Cut 1 strip 1½" x 13" for the background bars (A).
• Cut 2 squares 2⅞" x 2⅞", then cut in half diagonally for the background triangles (B).

Fabric 3
• Cut 2 squares 2⅞" x 2⅞", then cut in half diagonally for the Monkey Wrench triangles (B).
• Cut 1 square 2½" x 2½" for the center square (C).

BLOCK ASSEMBLY

1. With right sides together, sew the Fabric 1 strip to the Fabric 2 strip. Press. Cut the strip set into 4 units, each 2½" wide.

2. Sew each Fabric 2 B triangle, right sides together, to a Fabric 3 B triangle. Press. Make 4.

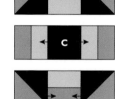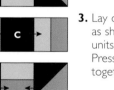

3. Lay out the block as shown. Sew the units into rows. Press. Sew the rows together. Press.

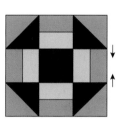

 ### Four-H Block
Finished block size: 6" x 6"

CUTTING

Fabric 1
• Cut 1 strip 1½" x 8" for the center square (A).

Fabric 2
• Cut 2 strips 1½" x 8" for the short logs (B).

Fabric 3
• Cut 1 strip 1½" x 32", then cut into 8 rectangles 1½" x 3½" for the long logs (C).

BLOCK ASSEMBLY

1. With right sides together, sew a B strip to each long edge of the A strip. Press. Cut the strip set into 4 segments, each 1½" wide.

2. Sew C rectangles to opposite sides of each unit from Step 1. Press. Make 4.

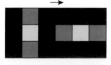

3. Lay out the block as shown, carefully turning the units. Sew the units into rows. Press. Sew the rows together. Press.

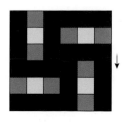

Blocks with Pieced Triangles

If you've been a little nervous about piecing blocks with lots of triangles, give these blocks a try. You'll get lots of practice piecing triangles, both large and small, and you'll love the finished results in your quilts!

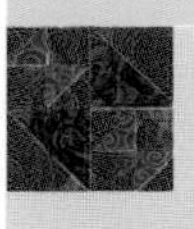

Crosses and Losses Block
Finished block size: 6" x 6"

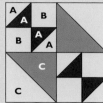

CUTTING

Fabric 1
- Cut 2 squares 2⅜" x 2⅜", then cut in half diagonally for the small triangles (A).

Fabric 2
- Cut 2 squares 2⅜" x 2⅜", then cut in half diagonally for the small background triangles (A).

- Cut 4 squares 2" x 2" for the background squares (B).
- Cut 1 square 3⅞" x 3⅞", then cut in half diagonally for the large background triangles (C).

Fabric 3
- Cut 1 square 3⅞" x 3⅞", then cut in half diagonally for the large triangles (C).

BLOCK ASSEMBLY

1. Sew each Fabric 1 A triangle, right sides together, to a Fabric 2 A triangle. Press. Make 4.

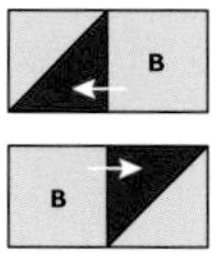

2. Lay out and sew the units from Step 1 and the B squares as shown. Press. Make 2.

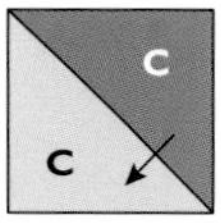

3. Sew each Fabric 2 C triangle, right sides together, to a Fabric 3 C triangle. Press. Make 2.

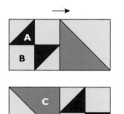

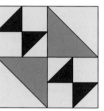

4. Lay out the block as shown. Sew the units into rows. Press. Sew the rows together. Press.

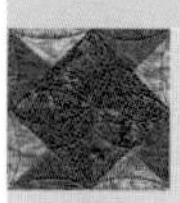

Unknown Block
Finished block size: 6" x 6"

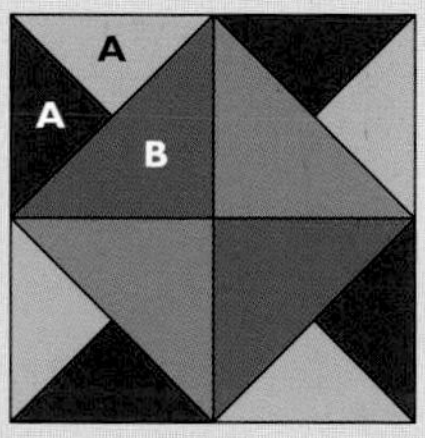

CUTTING

Fabric 1
- Cut 1 square 4¼" x 4¼", then cut in half diagonally in both directions for the small triangles (A).

Fabric 2
- Cut 1 square 4¼" x 4¼", then cut in half diagonally in both directions for the small triangles (A).

Fabric 3
- Cut 1 square 3⅞" x 3⅞", then cut in half diagonally for the large triangles (B).

Fabric 4
- Cut 1 square 3⅞" x 3⅞", then cut in half diagonally for the large triangles (B).

BLOCK ASSEMBLY

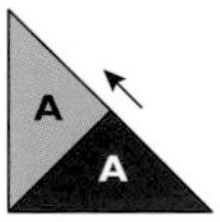

1. Sew each Fabric 1 A triangle, right sides together, to a Fabric 2 A triangle. Press. Make 4.

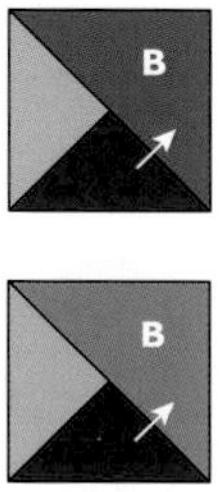

2. Sew a unit from Step 1 to each Fabric 3 and Fabric 4 B triangle. Press. Make 2 of each.

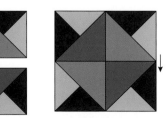

3. Lay out the block as shown. Sew the units into rows. Press. Sew the rows together. Press.

Blocks with Matching Points

These simple blocks will give you practice making triangles with perfect points, whether the points are in the center of the block, inside the block, or along the block edges.

Square-in-a-Square Block
Finished block size: 6" x 6"

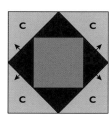

CUTTING

Fabric 1
- Cut 1 square 3½" x 3½" for the center square (A).

Fabric 2
- Cut 2 squares 3" x 3", then cut in half diagonally for the inner triangles (B).

Fabric 3
- Cut 2 squares 3⅞" x 3⅞", then cut in half diagonally for the corner triangles (C).

BLOCK ASSEMBLY

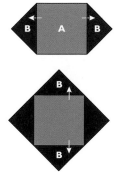

1. Fold the square in half vertically and horizontally to find midpoints along each edge. Fold the triangle in half to find the midpoint of the long edge. Match midpoints, and sew a B triangle to opposite sides of the A square. Press. Sew a B triangle to the remaining sides of the square. Press.

2. Repeat Step 1 to sew a C triangle to each side of the block. Refer to Pinning (page 9). With the A/B unit on top of a C triangle, sew the seam so the tip of A remains sharp. Press.

Pinwheel Block
Finished block size: 6" x 6"

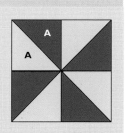

CUTTING

Fabric 1
- Cut 2 squares 3⅞" x 3⅞", then cut in half diagonally for the pinwheel (A).
- Option: Cut 1 square each from 2 different fabrics for pinwheel (A).

Fabric 2
- Cut 2 squares 3⅞" x 3⅞", then cut in half diagonally for the background (A).

BLOCK ASSEMBLY

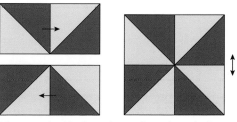

1. Sew a Fabric 1 A triangle, right sides together, to each Fabric 2 A triangle. Press. Make 4.

2. Lay out the block as shown. Sew the units into rows. Press. Refer to Pinning (page 9). Match the center intersection, pin, and sew the rows together. Press the center seam open.

Blocks with Sew-and-Flip Squares

This is the same technique as one I've shared for piecing the star points on the Sawtooth Star blocks (Method 2: Sew and Flip, page 14). You'll use it here to piece these blocks.

This method saves you the bother of cutting and sewing triangles and dealing with their bias edges. You can use it almost any time you need to sew a half-square triangle onto another larger piece to make a square or rectangular unit.

Snowball Block

Finished block size: 6" x 6"

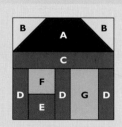

CUTTING

Fabric 1
• Cut 1 square 6½" x 6½" for the block center (A).

Fabric 2
• Cut 4 squares 2½" x 2½" for the block corners (B).

BLOCK ASSEMBLY

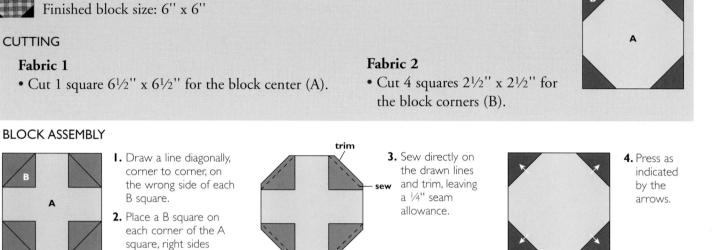

1. Draw a line diagonally, corner to corner, on the wrong side of each B square.

2. Place a B square on each corner of the A square, right sides together.

trim

sew

3. Sew directly on the drawn lines and trim, leaving a ¼" seam allowance.

4. Press as indicated by the arrows.

House Block

Finished block size: 6" x 6"

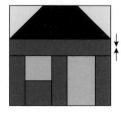

CUTTING

Fabric 1
• Cut 1 rectangle 2½" x 6½" for the roof (A).
Fabric 2
• Cut 2 squares 2½" x 2½" for the sky (B).
Fabric 3
• Cut 1 strip 1½" x 20", then cut into 1 rectangle 1½" x 6½" (C) and 3 rectangles 1½" x 3½" (D) for the house.
• Cut 1 square 2" x 2" for the house (E).

Fabric 4
• Cut 1 square 2" x 2" for the window (F).
• Cut 1 rectangle 2" x 3½" for the door (G).

BLOCK ASSEMBLY

1. Draw a line diagonally, corner to corner, on the wrong side of each B square.

2. Align a B square with each short edge of A, right sides together.

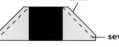

trim

sew

3. Sew directly on the drawn lines and trim, leaving a ¼" seam allowance.

4. Press as indicated by the arrows.

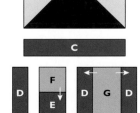

5. Lay out and sew the block. Press.

Blocks with Partial Seams

Wrap strips, triangles, or other shapes around a center square with this nifty piecing technique. It's easy! You'll stop just short of completing the seam that joins the first element to the center square, work your way around the block clockwise to add the remaining elements, and then go back to complete the first seam.

Bright Hopes Block

Finished block size: 6" x 6"

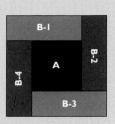

CUTTING

Fabric 1
- Cut 1 square 3½" x 3½" for the center square (A).

Fabric 2
- Cut 4 strips 2" x 5" for the rectangles (B).
- Option: Cut the B rectangles from 2 or 4 different fabrics.

BLOCK ASSEMBLY

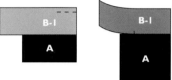

1. With right sides together, align the top edge of a B strip to the top edge of A. Sew the strip to the square. Stop stitching 1" from the bottom edge of the square. Press.

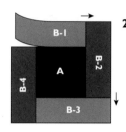

2. Sew a B strip to each remaining side of the unit from Step 1, in the order shown. Press.

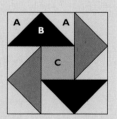

3. Complete the seam between B-1 and B-4. Press.

Night Vision Variation Block

Finished block size: 6" x 6"

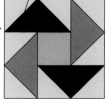

CUTTING

Refer to Method 1: Cutting Triangles (page 13).

Fabric 1
- Cut 4 squares 2⅞" x 2⅞", then cut in half diagonally for the background triangles (A).

Fabric 2
- Cut 1 square 5¼" x 5¼", then cut in half diagonally in both directions. You'll need 2 quarter-square triangles for the large triangles (B).

Fabric 3
- Cut 1 square 5¼" x 5¼", then cut in half diagonally in both directions. You'll need 2 quarter-square triangles for the large triangles (B).

Fabric 4
- Cut 1 square 2½" x 2½" for the center square (C).

BLOCK ASSEMBLY

1. Sew A to a short side of each Fabric 2 and Fabric 3 B triangle. The ^ indicates which edge or point to line up. Press. Repeat on the other short side of each Fabric 2 and Fabric 3 B triangle. Press. Make 2 of each.

2. With right sides together, align the top edge of a Fabric 2 unit with the top edge of C. Sew the unit to the square. Stop stitching 1" from the bottom edge of the square. Press.

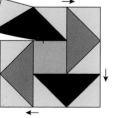

3. Working in a clockwise direction, sew a Fabric 3 unit, then a Fabric 2 unit, and then the remaining Fabric 3 unit to the unit from Step 2. Press.

4. Complete the seam between the first and last units added. Press.

Blocks with Y-Seams

Sometimes the piecing sequence for a block requires you to take a little detour in the seam so you can inset a neighboring piece. These Y-seams may seem tricky, but they're as simple as pie if you know the secret—and now you will! Simply mark a dot ¼" from the edge of one of the pieces at the point where the two neighboring pieces meet. Stitch to the point (dot), stop, and backstitch. Continue stitching the other seams in the same manner.

Basket Block
Finished block size: 6" x 6"

CUTTING

Fabric 1
- Cut 1 square 3¾" x 3¾", then cut in half diagonally in both directions. You'll need 2 quarter-square triangles for the background (A).
- Cut 1 square 2¼" x 2¼" for the background square (B).
- Cut 2 rectangles 2¼" x 3" for the background rectangles (F).
- Cut 1 square 4⅜" x 4⅜", then cut in half diagonally. You'll need 1 half-square triangle for the background (G).

Fabric 2
- Cut 4 rectangles (total) 1¾" x 4¼" for the diamonds (C).

Fabric 3
- Cut 1 square 3⅜" x 3⅜", then cut in half diagonally. You'll need 1 half-square triangle for the basket (D).
- Cut 1 square 2⅝" x 2⅝", then cut in half diagonally. You'll need both half-square triangles for the basket (E).

BLOCK ASSEMBLY

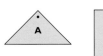

1. Mark a dot ¼" in from the 90° corner on the wrong side of A and on the wrong side in one corner of B.

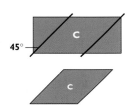

2. Trim both ends of C at parallel 45° angles.

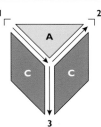

3. Lay out 2 C pieces and 1 A. The ^ indicates which edge or point to line up. Piece the unit in the sequence shown. Stop and backstitch at the dot.

4. Press seams A/C, following the arrows. Press seam C/C open. Make 2 units.

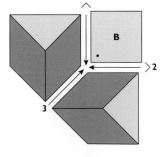

5. Lay out the 2 completed units from Step 4. Add B, sewing in the sequence shown and in the direction indicated by the arrows. Stop and backstitch at the dot. The ^ indicates which edge or point to line up.

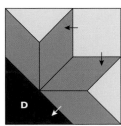

6. Sew D to the unit from Step 5. Press.

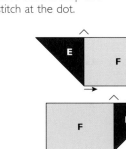

7. Sew E to F. The ^ indicates which edge or point to line up. Press. Make 1 of each.

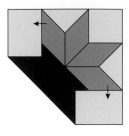

8. Sew the units from Step 7 to 2 sides of the unit from Step 6. Press.

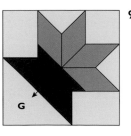

9. Sew G to the unit from Step 8. Press.

Spool Block
Finished block size: 6" x 6"

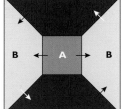

CUTTING

Fabric 1
- Cut 1 square 2½" x 2½" for the center square (A).

Fabric 2
- Cut 2 rectangles 2½" x 7¼" for the spool (B).

Fabric 3
- Cut 2 rectangles 2½" x 7¼" for the background (B).

BLOCK ASSEMBLY

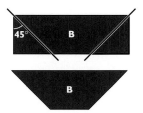

1. Trim both ends of each B rectangle at opposing 45° angles.

2. Mark a dot ¼" in from each corner on the wrong side of A. These are your stop/start points for the Y-seams.

3. With right sides together and starting with a backstitch at the dot, sew a Fabric 2 B piece to one side of A. Stop and backstitch at the dot at the opposite corner. The ˆ indicates which edge or point to line up. Repeat to sew the remaining Fabric 2 B piece to the opposite side of the square. Press.

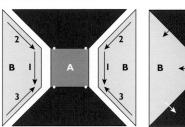

4. Sew a Fabric 3 B piece to the remaining sides of A. Sew in the sequence shown and in the direction indicated by the arrows. Stop and backstitch at each dot. Press.

Blocks with Diagonal Piecing

In these blocks, the rows appear on the diagonal and are finished with corner and/or side triangles. Never fear: you'll still be sewing simple rows; they just appear angled in the finished block. By the way, here's that bonus block you've been waiting for (Anvil block, page 22).

Crossroads Block
Finished block size: 6" x 6"

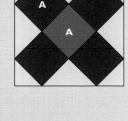

CUTTING

Fabric 1
- Cut 1 square 2⅝" x 2⅝" for the center square (A).

Fabric 2
- Cut 4 squares 2⅝" x 2⅝" for the surrounding squares (A).

Fabric 3
- Cut 1 square 4¼" x 4¼", then cut in half twice diagonally for the large background triangles (B).
- Cut 2 squares 2⅜" x 2⅜", then cut in half diagonally for the background corner triangles (C).

BLOCK ASSEMBLY

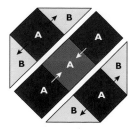

1. Lay out the Fabric 1 A squares and Fabric 2 A squares and the B triangles in rows. Sew the squares and triangles together in rows. Press.

2. Sew the rows together. Press.

3. Sew a C triangle to each corner. Press.

Anvil Block
Finished block size: 6" x 6"

CUTTING

Fabric 1
- Cut 1 square 2½" x 2½" for the center square (A).

Fabric 2
- Cut 2 squares 2⅞" x 2⅞", then cut in half diagonally for the small triangles (B).

Fabric 3
- Cut 2 squares 2½" x 2½" for the background squares (C).
- Cut 1 square 4⅞" x 4⅞", then cut in half diagonally for the background corner triangles (D).

BLOCK ASSEMBLY

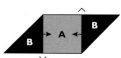

1. Sew B to opposite sides of A. The ^ indicates which edge or point to line up. Press.

2. Sew B to C. The ^ indicates which edge or point to line up. Press. Make 2.

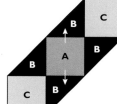

3. Lay out and sew together the units from Step 1 and Step 2. Press.

4. Sew D to opposite corners of the block. Press.

Mock Card Trick Block
Finished block size: 6" x 6"

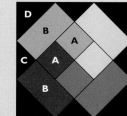

CUTTING

Fabric 1
- Cut 1 square 1⅞" x 1⅞" for the four patch (A).
- Cut 1 rectangle 2" x 3¼" for the bar (B).

Fabric 2
- Cut 1 square 1⅞" x 1⅞" for the four patch (A).
- Cut 1 rectangle 2" x 3¼" for the bar (B).

Fabric 3
- Cut 1 square 1⅞" x 1⅞" for the four patch (A).
- Cut 1 rectangle 2" x 3¼" for the bar (B).

Fabric 4
- Cut 1 square 1⅞" x 1⅞" for the four patch (A).
- Cut 1 rectangle 2" x 3¼" for the bar (B).

Fabric 5
- Cut 1 square 3¼" x 3¼", then cut in half diagonally in both directions for the small background triangles (C).
- Cut 2 squares 2⅞" x 2⅞", then cut in half diagonally for the corner background triangles (D).

BLOCK ASSEMBLY

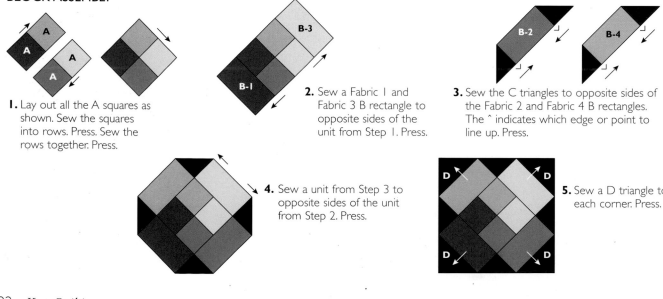

1. Lay out all the A squares as shown. Sew the squares into rows. Press. Sew the rows together. Press.

2. Sew a Fabric 1 and Fabric 3 B rectangle to opposite sides of the unit from Step 1. Press.

3. Sew the C triangles to opposite sides of the Fabric 2 and Fabric 4 B rectangles. The ^ indicates which edge or point to line up. Press.

4. Sew a unit from Step 3 to opposite sides of the unit from Step 2. Press.

5. Sew a D triangle to each corner. Press.

PROJECTS

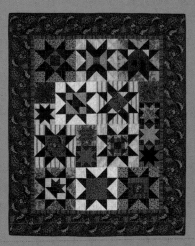

Autumn

Pieced and machine quilted by LeAnna Christopher, 2004.
Finished quilt size: 62½" x 62½"

Dynamite Design Options

LeAnna used a wonderful, multicolored, large-scale, floral-and-leaf print as her quilt's focus fabric. A warm, brown print made the perfect "go-with" choice for sashing, and the blocks were made from a variety of coordinating prints. Your palette will be directed by the focus fabric you select. Why not make your quilt the colors of your favorite season?

LeAnna repeated the same fabrics in each of the five large Sawtooth Star blocks. For a scrappier look, you can mix the fabrics from block to block. You can substitute a personal favorite block for the center square or use a different block for each if that's your wish.

The Sawtooth Star in this quilt alternates with a second block—each pieced from four assorted 6" blocks—in a simple sashed setting. Duplicate LeAnna's choices or select any combination of blocks that you'd like.

MATERIALS

Fabric amounts are based on a 42" fabric width.

- **Assorted cream, tan, pink, green, purple, and black prints:** 2½ yards total for blocks
- **Dark pink print:** ½ yard for Sawtooth Star block background
- **Cream print:** ⅓ yard for Sawtooth Star block star points
- **Coordinating brown print:** ¾ yard for sashing
- **Coordinating large-scale floral print:** 1⅞ yards for border
- **Dark brown print:** ½ yard for binding
- **Backing:** 3¾ yards
- **Batting:** 67" x 67"

CUTTING THE SASHING, BORDERS, AND BINDING

All measurements include a ¼" seam allowance.

Coordinating brown print
- Cut 9 strips 2½" x the fabric width for the sashing.

Coordinating large-scale floral print
- Cut 2 strips 9½" x 44½" on the lengthwise grain (parallel to the selvage) for the side borders.
- Cut 2 strips 9½" x 62½" on the lengthwise grain for the top and bottom borders.

Dark brown print
- Cut 7 strips 2⅛" x the fabric width for the binding.

STAR BLOCKS

1. Refer to Mock Card Trick Block (page 22). Cut and construct 5 Mock Card Trick Blocks using assorted cream, tan, and green prints.

Make 5.

2. Refer to 12" and 6" Sawtooth Star Blocks: Three Easy Methods (page 13). Choose the method you prefer for piecing the 12" Sawtooth Star Block. Cut the appropriate number of pieces in the sizes listed from the dark pink and cream prints to make 5 Sawtooth Star Blocks, 12" x 12" finished. Construct the blocks, using a block from Step 1 for the center square.

Make 5.

ALTERNATE BLOCKS

1. Refer to Block Instructions (pages 13–22) to cut and construct 1 each of the following blocks to make the quilt shown on page 24. Use the assorted cream, tan, pink, green, purple, and black prints. Feel free to substitute any of the blocks in Block Instructions for those listed below. I recommend choosing blocks from as many different categories as possible.

    Crossroads Block (page 21)
    Snowball Block (page 18)
    Four-H Block (page 15)
    Crosses and Losses Block (page 16)
    Spool Block (page 21)
    Unknown Block (page 16)
    Pinwheel Block (page 17)
    Square-in-a-Square Block (page 17)

2. Repeat Step 1 to make 2 each of the following blocks:

    Anvil Block (page 22)
    Night Vision Variation Block (page 19)
    Bright Hopes Block (page 19)
    Monkey Wrench Block (page 15)

3. Referring to the photo on page 24 and the assembly diagram on page 27 for guidance, arrange 4 blocks from Step 1 and Step 2 in 2 rows of 2 blocks each. Sew the blocks into rows. Press. Sew the rows together. Press. Make 4 blocks.

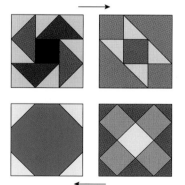 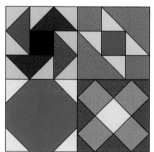

Make 4 alternate blocks.

QUILT ASSEMBLY

Refer to the photo on page 24 and the assembly diagram below for guidance as needed.

1. Join the 2½"-wide brown print strips together end to end with diagonal seams. From this strip, cut 6 strips 2½" x 12½", 4 strips 2½" x 40½", and 2 strips 2½" x 44½".

2. Lay out the Sawtooth Star Blocks, the alternate blocks, and the 2½" x 12½" brown print sashing strips in 3 rows, alternating the blocks. Two rows will have 2 Star blocks and 1 alternate block, and one row will have 2 alternate blocks and 1 Star block.

3. Sew the blocks and sashing strips into rows. Press.

4. Lay out the 2½" x 40½" brown print sashing strips and the rows from Step 3, alternating them as shown in the assembly diagram. Sew the sashing strips and rows together. Press the seams toward the sashing strips.

5. Sew the 2½" x 44½" brown print sashing strips to the top and bottom of the unit from Step 4. Press the seams toward the sashing strips.

6. Sew the 9½"-wide large-scale floral print border strips to the sides, top, and bottom of the quilt. Press the seams toward the border strips.

FINISHING

Follow the General Instructions (pages 11–12) to layer, baste, and quilt your quilt. Sew together the 2⅛"-wide brown print strips end to end with diagonal seams and use them to bind the edges.

> **LeAnna's Tip** Sometimes the quilt determines what works—both technically and visually—as you lay out the blocks. Don't be afraid to discard an already-finished block if it doesn't fit into your quilt. You can put an extra block to many uses—for example, as a signature block on the back of the quilt. You can even slip a block into a thank-you note to a special friend.

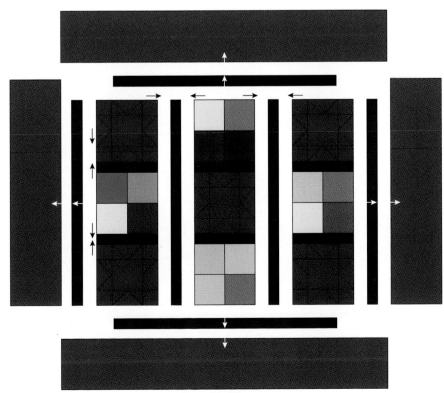

Assembly Diagram

Basket Bouquet

Pieced by Dee Christopher, machine quilted by Faye Collinsworth, 2004.
Finished quilt size: 60½" × 60½"

Dynamite Design Options

Dee's fabrics are a feminine blend of soft pinks, greens, and neutrals in a wonderful range of size and scale of print. A dreamy, cottage-style floral print completes the look in the sashing and borders. You can, of course, substitute any palette you wish.

The Sawtooth Star Blocks and the blocks Dee chose for their centers are a visually pleasing, scrappy mix that you can choose to duplicate or change as you please.

Basket Bouquet draws its name from the eight 6" Basket Blocks Dee used for the sashing cornerstones and in the four corners of her quilt. Not only did she use the same block for this important design element, but she also chose to make them all in the same fabrics.

The sashing strips were cut 6½" wide to accommodate the cornerstones, but you can adjust the width by eliminating the blocks or by replacing them with simple fabric squares. Because she used the identical fabric for both sashing strips and borders, Dee's blocks appear to float over the quilt surface. A different fabric here could minimize or eliminate that effect, or—depending on the fabric you choose—it could create a frame around each block.

MATERIALS

Fabric amounts are based on a 42" fabric width.

- **Assorted cream, tan, green, pink, and purple prints:** 3½ yards total for blocks
- **Light floral print:** 2¼ yards for sashing and border
- **Dark print:** ½ yard for binding
- **Backing:** 3⅔ yards
- **Batting:** 65" x 65"

CUTTING THE SASHING, BORDERS, AND BINDING

All measurements include a ¼" seam allowance.

Light floral print

- Cut 4 strips 6½" x the fabric width on the crosswise grain (selvage to selvage); crosscut into 12 strips 6½" x 12½" for the sashing.
- Cut 4 strips 6½" x 48½" on the lengthwise grain (parallel to the selvage) for the borders.

Dark print

- Cut 7 strips 2⅛" x the fabric width for the binding.

STAR BLOCKS

1. Refer to Block Instructions (pages 13–22) to cut and construct 1 each of the following blocks to make the quilt shown on page 28. Use the assorted cream, tan, green, pink, and purple prints. Feel free to substitute any of the blocks in Block Instructions for those listed below. I suggest choosing blocks from as many different categories as possible.

   Crosses and Losses Block (page 16)
   Night Vision Variation Block (page 19)
   Anvil Block (page 22)
   Monkey Wrench Block (page 15)
   Square-in-a-Square Block (page 17)
   Crossroads Block (page 21)
   Snowball Block (page 18)
   Unknown Block (page 16)
   Bright Hopes Block (page 19)

2. Refer to 12" and 6" Sawtooth Star Blocks: Three Easy Methods (page 13). Choose the method you prefer for piecing the 12" Sawtooth Star Block. Cut the appropriate number of pieces in the sizes listed from the assorted cream, tan, green, pink, and purple prints to make 9 Sawtooth Star Blocks, 12" x 12" finished. Construct the blocks, using a block from Step 1 for the center square.

Make 9, each with a different center block.

BASKET BLOCKS

Refer to Basket Block (page 20). Cut and construct 8 Basket blocks using assorted pink and green prints.

Make 8.

QUILT ASSEMBLY

Refer to the photo on page 28 and the assembly diagram on page 31 for guidance as needed.

1. Sew together 2 Basket Blocks and 3 light floral print 6½" x 12½" sashing strips. Press. Make 2.

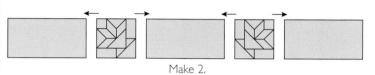

Make 2.

2. Sew together 2 light floral print 6½" x 12½" sashing strips and 3 Star Blocks. Press. Make 3.

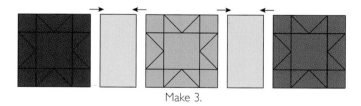

Make 3.

3. Lay out the units from Step 1 and the rows from Step 2 as shown in the assembly diagram. Sew the rows together. Press.

4. Sew a light floral print border strip to opposite sides of the quilt. Press the seams toward the border strips.

5. Sew a Basket Block to each end of a remaining light floral print 6½" x 48½" border strip. Press. Make 2.

Make 2.

6. Sew a border unit from Step 5 to the top and bottom of the quilt. Press.

FINISHING

Follow the General Instructions (pages 11–12) to layer, baste, and quilt your quilt. Sew together the 2⅛"-wide dark strips end to end with diagonal seams, and use them to bind the edges.

Dee's Tip Often, it is better not to match fabrics too closely. Even the slightest variations in color can turn a beautiful quilt into a stunning quilt. Don't be afraid to experiment with fabric. The more you play, the more confident you will become.

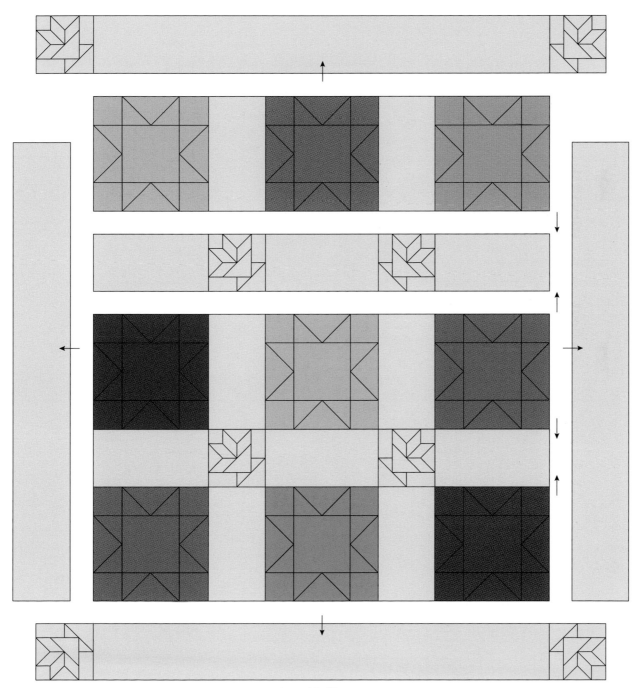

Assembly Diagram

It's Harvest Time

Pieced and machine quilted by Paula Reid, 2004.
Finished quilt size: 57¾'' × 57¾''

Dynamite Design Options

In this quilt, Paula used a minimum number of large Sawtooth Star Blocks for maximum impact. She turned four sashed blocks on point to create a fabulous overall square-in-a-square setting. Then she finished the quilt with dramatic dark setting triangles, clever (and easy-to-piece) inner and outer borders, and a middle border dressed with four 6" pieced corner squares. You can use the same blocks that Paula selected, or you can choose your favorites to create a customized design.

This is a great quilt for using all of those glorious batiks and precious hand-dyed fabrics you've been eyeing at the quilt shop. Paula used the same black (from P&B Textiles) and light-yellow hand-dyes for the background and points of the Sawtooth Stars, but you can make your own decision about how scrappy you'd like to go. Look for a great multicolored focus fabric for the sashing and outer border—this quilt uses a rich multicolored batik print—to pull it all together.

MATERIALS

Fabric amounts are based on a 42" fabric width.

- **Assorted purple, yellow, gold, and rust hand-dyed and batik fabrics and black:** 1⅛ yards total for blocks
- **Black fabric:** 1¾ yards for Sawtooth Star block background and large setting triangles
- **Light yellow hand-dyed fabric:** ⅓ yard for Sawtooth Star block star points
- **Coordinating multicolored batik print:** 1⅜ yards for sashing and middle border
- **Assorted yellow and gold hand-dyed fabrics:** ⅞ yard total for pieced inner and outer borders
- **Purple hand-dyed or batik fabric:** ½ yard for binding
- **Backing:** 3½ yards
- **Batting:** 62" x 62"

CUTTING THE SASHING, BORDERS, AND BINDING

All measurements include a ¼" seam allowance.

Black hand-dyed fabric

- Cut 2 squares 21½" x 21½", then cut each square in half once diagonally to make 2 setting triangles (4 total).

Coordinating multicolored batik print

- Cut 5 strips 2¼" x the fabric width for the sashing, then cut:

    2 strips 2¼" x 12½"

    3 strips 2¼" x 26¼"

    2 strips 2¼" x 29¾"

- Cut 4 strips 6½" x 42" for the middle border.

Assorted yellow and gold hand-dyed fabrics

- Cut 12 strips (total) 2¼" x the fabric width for the pieced inner and outer borders.

Purple hand-dyed or batik fabric

- Cut 7 strips 2⅛" x the fabric width for the binding.

STAR BLOCKS

1. Refer to Block Instructions (pages 13–22) to cut and construct 1 each of the following blocks to make the quilt shown. Use the assorted purple, yellow, gold, rust, and black hand-dyed and batik fabrics. Feel free to substitute any of the blocks in Block Instructions for those listed below. I recommend choosing blocks from as many different categories as possible.

    Square-in-a-Square Block (page 17)
    Monkey Wrench Block (page 15)
    Basket Block (page 20)
    Bright Hopes Block (page 19)

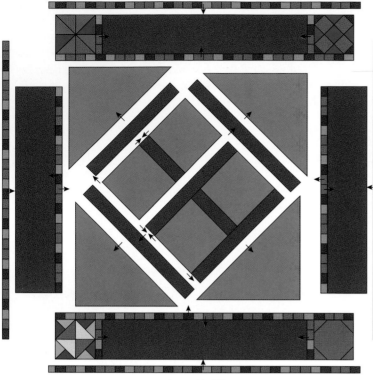

Assembly Diagram

2. Refer to 12" and 6" Sawtooth Star Blocks: Three Easy Methods (page 13). Choose the method you prefer for piecing the 12" Sawtooth Star Block. Cut the appropriate number of pieces in the sizes listed from the black and light yellow hand-dyed fabrics to make 4 Sawtooth Star Blocks, 12" x 12" finished.

Make 4, each with a different center block.

CUTTING AND MAKING THE CORNER BLOCKS

Refer to Block Instructions (pages 13–22) to cut and construct 1 each of the following blocks to make the

corner squares for the outer border. Use the assorted purple, yellow, gold, rust, and black fabrics. Feel free to substitute any of the blocks in Block Instructions for those listed below. I recommend choosing blocks from as many different categories as possible.

Pinwheel Block (page 17)
Crossroads Block (page 21)
Unknown Block (page 16)
Snowball Block (page 18)

QUILT ASSEMBLY

Refer to the photo on page 32 and the assembly diagram for guidance as needed.

1. Sew a multicolored batik 2¼" x 12½" sashing strip between 2 star blocks. Press the seams toward the sashing strip. Make 2.

2. Lay out the 2¼" x 26¼" multicolored batik sashing strips and the rows from Step 1, alternating them as shown in the assembly diagram. Sew the sashing strips and rows together. Press the seams toward the sashing strips.

3. Sew the 2¼" x 29¾" multicolored batik sashing strips to the sides of the unit from Step 2. Press the seams toward the sashing strips.

4. Sew a large black hand-dyed triangle piece to opposite sides of the unit from Step 3. Press the seams toward the triangles. Sew a black triangle to the remaining sides. Press.

BORDERS

1. With right sides together, sew together 4 assorted yellow and gold hand-dyed 2¼"-wide fabric strips. Press. Make 3 strip sets. Cut the strip sets into 66 segments total, each 1½" wide.

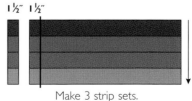

Make 3 strip sets.
Cut 66 segments.

2. Sew together 6 segments from Step 1 end to end to make a continuous 1½"-wide pieced inner border strip. Press. Make 2.

3. Sew 8 segments from Step 1 together end to end to make a continuous 1½"-wide pieced inner border strip. Press. Make 2. Set the remaining segments aside for now.

4. Measure the quilt top through the center from top to bottom. Trim the pieced inner border strips you made in Step 2 and all 4 of the 6½"-wide multi-colored batik middle border strips to this measurement. Sew a pieced inner border strip and a 6½"-wide batik middle border strip together to make a side border unit. Press the seams toward the middle border strip. Make 2.

5. Referring to the photo and assembly diagram for guidance, sew a border unit from Step 4 to the sides of the quilt. Press the seams away from the border units.

6. Measure the quilt top through the center from side to side, including the border units you added in Step 5. Trim the pieced inner border strips you made in Step 3 to this measurement.

7. Trim each of the 4 remaining pieced inner border segments you cut in Step 1 to 6½". Sew a strip to each corner block. Press.

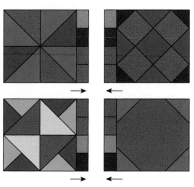

Make 1 of each.

8. Referring to the photo and assembly diagram for guidance, sew a corner block from Step 7 to both ends of a 6½"-wide batik middle border strip. Press the seams toward the border unit. Make 2.

9. Sew a pieced inner border strip from Step 6 and the unit from Step 8 together to make a top/bottom border unit. Press the seams toward the outer border strips. Make 2. Sew them to the top and bottom of the quilt. Press the seams away from the border units.

10. Sew 8 units from Step 1 together end to end to make a continuous 1½"-wide pieced outer side border strip. Press. Make 2.

11. Measure the quilt top through the center from top to bottom. Trim the pieced outer border strips you made in Step 10 to this measurement. Sew the strips to the sides of the quilt. Press the seams toward the middle border.

12. Sew 9 units from Step 1 together end to end to make a continuous 1½"-wide pieced outer top/bottom border strip. Press. Make 2.

13. Measure the quilt top through the center from side to side. Trim the pieced outer border strips you made in Step 12 to this measurement. Sew the strips to the top and bottom of the quilt. Press seams toward the middle border.

FINISHING

Follow the General Instructions (pages 11–12) to layer, baste, and quilt your quilt. Sew the 2⅛"-wide purple hand-dyed or batik strips together end to end with diagonal seams, and use them to bind the edges.

Paula's Tip Wash your bound quilt in plain cold water on the gentle cycle. Don't use the soak cycle, as some agitation is needed to ensure removal of any chemical residue from the fabric or from the marking tool you've used. Since I don't prewash my fabrics, I take the additional precaution of dropping a dye-trapping sheet into the washing machine with my quilt. This product—available at grocery stores—is a disposable, paperlike sheet that absorbs any excess color released into the water.

Crop Circles

Pieced and machine quilted by Cheryl Uribe, 2004.
Finished quilt size: 63½" × 63½"

Dynamite Design Options

The terrific green circle print Cheryl selected for her outer border fabric not only makes the ideal frame for the sixteen vividly colored Sawtooth Star Blocks but also inspired both the quilting design (see Cheryl's Tip on page 39) and the name for her quilt.

Cheryl went all out with both the block centers—she used all but one of the 6" block options—and the color. You can choose an equally vibrant, jewel-like palette, or you can substitute a personal favorite collection of soft pastels, bright primary colors, or rich earth tones. The choice of blocks is up to you as well. You can run the gamut, as Cheryl did, or choose just a few favorite blocks.

By setting the blocks side by side without sashing, Cheryl created a sparkling overall quilt design. Secondary images of scrappy four patches and colorful split diamonds pop up everywhere, an effect she's encouraged with the variety of Star backgrounds.

A narrow inner border makes the Star Blocks seem to float in the center area of the quilt and provides a nice break between the center action and the checkerboard-style border that Cheryl pieced from the leftover prints. You can substitute a plain border if you prefer, but then you'd miss so much of the fun of this fabulous quilt. In fact, Cheryl had so much fun (including quilting the quilt in variegated thread), she offers a bonus tip on page 39.

MATERIALS

Fabric amounts are based on a 42" fabric width.

- **Assorted bright yellow, yellow-green, green, blue, pink, and purple prints:** 5⅓ yards total for blocks and pieced border
- **Bright yellow-green print:** ¼ yard for inner border
- **Green circle print:** 1⅞ yards for outer border
- **Dark print:** ½ yard for binding
- **Backing:** 4 yards
- **Batting:** 68" x 68"

CUTTING THE SASHING, BORDERS, AND BINDING

All measurements include a ¼" seam allowance.

Assorted bright yellow, yellow-green, green, blue, pink, and purple prints

- Cut 16 strips 1½" x the fabric width for the pieced border.

Bright yellow-green print

- Cut 5 strips 1" x the fabric width for the inner border.

Green circle print

- Cut 2 strips 5½" x 53½" on the lengthwise grain (parallel to the selvage) for the outer side borders.
- Cut 2 strips 5½" x 63½" on the lengthwise grain for the outer top and bottom borders.

Dark print

- Cut 7 strips 2⅛" x the fabric width for the binding.

STAR BLOCKS

1. Refer to Block Instructions (pages 13–22) to cut and construct 1 each of the following blocks to make the quilt shown on page 36. Use the assorted bright yellow, yellow-green, green, blue, pink, and purple prints. Feel free to substitute any of the blocks in Block Instructions for those listed below. I recommend choosing blocks from as many different categories as possible.

> Pinwheel Block (page 17)
> Basket Block (page 20)
> Four-H Block (page 15)
> Spool Block (page 21)
> Monkey Wrench Block (page 15)
> Unknown Block (page 16)
> 6" Sawtooth Star Block (page 13)
> Anvil Block (page 22)
> House Block (page 18)
> Mock Card Trick Block (page 22)
> Night Vision Variation Block (page 19)
> Square-in-a-Square Block (page 17)
> Snowball Block (page 18)
> Crosses and Losses Block (page 16)

2. Repeat Step 1 to make 2 Bright Hopes blocks (page 19).

3. Refer to 12" and 6" Sawtooth Star Blocks: Three Easy Methods (page 13). Choose the method you prefer for piecing the 12" Sawtooth Star Block. Cut the appropriate number of pieces in the sizes listed from the bright yellow, yellow-green, green, blue, pink, and purple prints to make 16 Sawtooth Star Blocks, 12" x 12" finished. Construct the blocks, using a block from Step 1 or Step 2 for the center square.

Make 16.

QUILT ASSEMBLY

Refer to the photo on page 36 and the assembly diagram for guidance as needed.

1. Arrange and sew the blocks in a pleasing arrangement of 4 horizontal rows of 4 blocks each. Press the seams in alternate rows in opposite directions.

2. Sew the rows together. Press.

BORDERS

1. Join the 1"-wide bright yellow-green print strips together end to end with a diagonal seam. Measure the quilt top through the center from top to bottom, then trim the inner border strips to this measurement. Sew the strips to the sides of the quilt. Press the seams toward the inner border strips.

2. Measure the quilt top through the center from side to side, including the inner border strips. Trim the top and bottom inner border strips to this measurement. Sew the strips to the top and bottom of the quilt. Press the seams toward the inner border strips.

3. With right sides together, sew 2 assorted bright yellow, yellow-green, green, blue, pink, and purple 1½"-wide strips together. Press. Make 8 strip sets. Cut the strip sets into 204 segments, each 1½" wide.

1½"

Make 8 strip sets. Cut 204 segments.

4. Sew together 49 assorted segments from Step 2 to make a pieced border strip. Press. Make 2. Sew the strips to opposite sides of the quilt. Press the seams away from the pieced border strips.

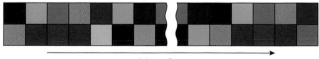

Make 2.

5. Repeat Step 3 to make 2 pieced border strips, each with 53 segments. Press. Sew the strips to the top and bottom of the quilt. Press.

6. Sew the 5½"-wide green circle print outer border strips to the sides, top, and bottom of the quilt. Press the seams toward the outer border strips.

FINISHING

Follow the General Instructions (pages 11–12) to layer, baste, and quilt your quilt. Sew the 2⅛"-wide dark print strips together end to end with diagonal seams, and use them to bind the edges.

Cheryl's Tip When you can't decide on a quilting design to use on your quilt, take a clue from your focus fabric. The fabulous border print I used for this quilt, with its vibrant circular motif, was the perfect springboard for the quilting design.

Cheryl's Bonus Tip When you machine quilt with variegated thread, the change in color can make backstitched stops and starts very noticeable. Use very small stitches for your stops and starts, or eliminate the problem completely by tying and burying the thread tails between the layers of the quilt.

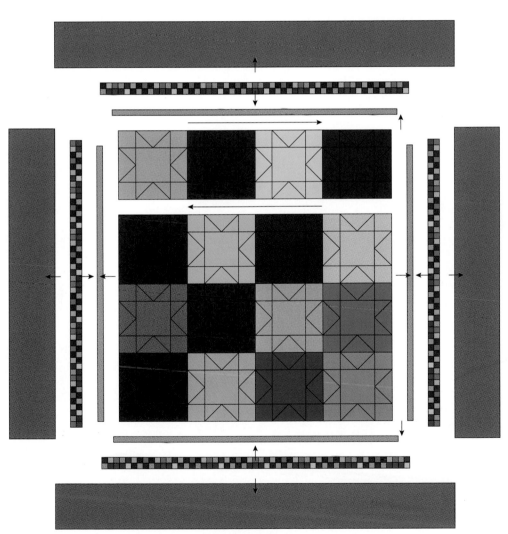

Assembly Diagram

Check and Balance

Pieced and machine quilted by Elizabeth Scott, 2004.
Finished quilt size: 50½" × 62½"

Dynamite Design Options

No doubt about it, the setting is the "star" in Elizabeth's quilt! Choosing to dispense with sashing, Elizabeth created a dynamic overall design by introducing a half-dozen 6" scrappy Sawtooth Stars as setting elements. Because the smaller blocks are half-sized versions of their also-scrappy 12" cousins, you'll find it easy to rearrange them to create your own unique setting.

Elizabeth used lots of plaids, stripes, and other geometric prints in her largely green, pink, and neutral palette—a strategy she encourages you to try as well. (See Elizabeth's Tip on page 43.) She likes the look of a striped fabric for an inner border (as do I—see *Tutti Frutti* on page 44), and she frames her quilt with a sumptuous green, large-scale floral. If you are uncertain about the color and fabric direction for your quilt, choose a knock-your-socks-off focal fabric, and use that as your guide.

MATERIALS

Fabric amounts are based on a 42" fabric width.

- **Assorted cream, tan, pink, rose, and green prints:** 3¼ yards total for blocks
- **Pink-and-green stripe:** ⅓ yard for inner border
- **Green large-scale floral print:** 1½ yards for outer border
- **Dark pink print:** ½ yard for binding
- **Backing:** 3⅛ yards
- **Batting:** 55" x 67"

CUTTING THE SASHING, BORDERS, AND BINDING

All measurements include a ¼" seam allowance.

Pink-and-green stripe

- Cut 5 strips 1½" x the fabric width for the inner border.

Green large-scale floral print

- Cut 4 strips 6½" x 50½" on the lengthwise grain (parallel to the selvage) for the outer border.

Dark pink print

- Cut 7 strips 2⅛" x the fabric width for the binding.

LARGE SAWTOOTH STAR BLOCKS

1. Refer to Block Instructions (pages 13–22) to cut and construct 1 each of the following blocks to make the quilt shown on page 40. Use the assorted cream, tan, pink, rose, and green prints. Feel free to substitute any of the blocks in Block Instructions for those listed below. I recommend choosing blocks from as many different categories as possible.

   Square-in-a-Square Block (page 17)
   Spool Block (page 21)
   House Block (page 18)
   Anvil Block (page 22)
   Unknown Block (page 16)
   Snowball Block (page 18)
   Monkey Wrench Block (page 15)
   Basket Block (page 20)
   Pinwheel Block (page 17)
   Bright Hopes Block (page 19)

2. Refer to 12" and 6" Sawtooth Star Blocks: Three Easy Methods (page 13). Choose the method you prefer for piecing the 12" Sawtooth Star Block. Cut the appropriate number of pieces in the sizes listed from the assorted cream, tan, pink, rose, and green prints to make 10 Sawtooth Star Blocks, 12" x 12" finished. Construct the blocks, using a block from Step 1 for the center square.

Make 10, each with a different center block.

CUTTING AND MAKING THE SMALL STAR BLOCKS

Refer to 12" and 6" Sawtooth Star Blocks: Three Easy Methods (page 13). Choose the method you prefer for piecing the 6" Sawtooth Star block. Cut the appropriate number of pieces in the sizes listed from the assorted cream, tan, pink, rose, and green prints to make 8 Sawtooth Star Blocks, 6" x 6" finished.

Make 8.

QUILT ASSEMBLY

Refer to the photo on page 40 and the assembly diagram for guidance as needed.

1. Lay out the blocks in a pleasing arrangement of 4 horizontal rows.

2. Sew the small Sawtooth Stars Blocks in Row 2 and Row 3 in pairs. Press.

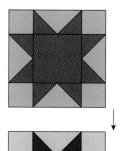
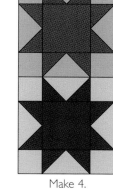

Make 4.

3. Sew the large and small Sawtooth Star Blocks into horizontal rows. Press the seams in opposite directions in alternate rows.

4. Sew the rows together. Press.

BORDERS

1. Join the 1½"-wide pink-and-green stripe strips together end to end. Measure the quilt top through the center from the top to bottom, then trim 2 inner border strips to this measurement. Sew the strips to the sides of the quilt. Press the seams toward the inner border strips.

2. Measure the quilt top through the center from side to side, including the inner border strips. Trim the 1½"-wide pieced border strip to this measurement. Make 2. Sew the strips to the top and bottom of the quilt. Press.

3. Sew the 6½"-wide green large-scale floral print outer border strips to the sides, top, and bottom of the quilt. Press the seams toward the outer border strips.

FINISHING

Follow the General Instructions (pages 11–12) to layer, baste, and quilt your quilt. Sew the 2⅛"-wide dark pink strips together end to end with diagonal seams, and use them to bind the edges.

Elizabeth's Tip Don't be afraid to use plaid and striped fabrics. They add a wonderful graphic dimension to your quilts. When cutting, follow the line of the design rather than the grainline of the fabric. Working with these fabrics requires a little more attention and planning, but the end result is well worth it. You can't make an exciting quilt without taking some chances!

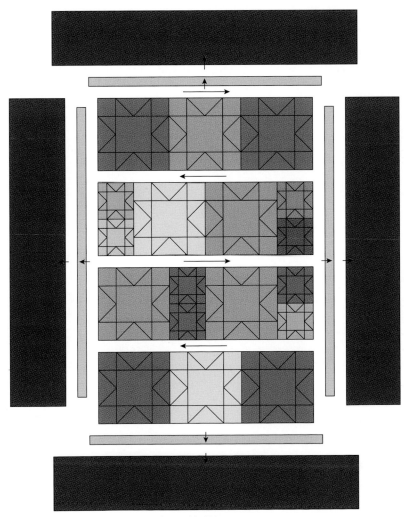

Assembly Diagram

Tutti Frutti

Pieced by Alex Anderson, machine quilted by Paula Reid, 2004.
Finished quilt size: 58½" × 58½"

Dynamite Design Options

Don't you just love the funky, 1950s-style print I found for the outer border of this quilt? The bright primary colors were the ideal match for the red, yellow, and blue prints I chose for the Sawtooth Star Blocks and their various 6" "bellies." (By the way, I thought of calling this book Star Bellies. Obviously cooler heads prevailed!) Although I chose fruit, you can easily substitute any theme for your focal fabric and go from there in making your subsequent fabric selections.

I made all of my large stars with blue points and blue-and-white backgrounds, but I cut them from different prints. And while all of my sashing strips are yellow, I cut them from two different prints: a fat, happy check for the inner sashes and a soft mottled print for the outer ones. You can follow my lead—or not!—whichever suits your fancy.

MATERIALS

Fabric amounts are based on a 42" fabric width.

- **Assorted blue, red, yellow, and blue-and-white prints:** 2⅔ yards total for blocks
- **Blue print:** ⅝ yard for cornerstones and binding
- **Yellow prints:** ⅜ yard each of 2 different fabrics for sashing
- **Blue-and-white stripe:** ⅓ yard for inner border
- **Coordinating multicolored fruit print:** 1⅔ yards for outer border
- **Backing:** 3⅝ yards
- **Batting:** 63" x 63"

CUTTING THE SASHING, BORDERS, AND BINDING

All measurements include a ¼" seam allowance.

Yellow prints

- Cut 4 strips 2½" x the fabric width from each fabric (8 total), then cut into 12 strips 2½" x 12½" (24 total) for the sashing.

Blue print

- Cut 1 strip 2½" x the fabric width, then cut into 16 squares 2½" x 2½" for the cornerstones.
- Cut 7 strips 2⅛" x the fabric width for the binding.

Blue-and-white stripe

- Cut 5 strips 1½" x the fabric width for the inner border.

Coordinating multicolored fruit print

- Cut 2 strips 6½" x 46½" on the lengthwise grain (parallel to the selvage) for the outer side borders.
- Cut 2 strips 6½" x 58½" on the lengthwise grain for the outer top and bottom borders.

STAR BLOCKS

1. Refer to Block Instructions (pages 13–22) to cut and construct 1 each of the following blocks to make the quilt shown on page 44. Use the assorted blue, red, yellow, and blue-and-white prints. Feel free to substitute any of the blocks in Block Instructions for those listed below. I recommend choosing blocks from as many different categories as possible.

> Mock Card Trick Block (page 22)
> 6" Sawtooth Star Block (page 13)
> Pinwheel Block (page 17)
> Snowball Block (page 18)
> Square-in-a-Square Block (page 17)
> House Block (page 18)
> Bright Hopes Block (page 19)
> Spool Block (page 21)
> Monkey Wrench Block (page 15)

2. Refer to 12" and 6" Sawtooth Star Blocks: Three Easy Methods (page 13). Choose the method you prefer for piecing the 12" Sawtooth Star Block. Cut the appropriate number of pieces in the sizes listed from the blue and blue-and-white prints to make 9 Sawtooth Star Blocks, 12" x 12" finished. Construct the blocks, using a block from Step 1 for the center square.

Make 9, each with a different center block.

QUILT ASSEMBLY

Refer to the photo on page 44 and the assembly diagram on page 47 for guidance as needed.

1. Sew together 4 blue print 2½" squares and 3 yellow print 2½" x 12½" strips. Press. Make 4.

Make 4.

2. Sew together 4 yellow print 2½" x 12½" strips and 3 blocks. Press. Make 3 rows.

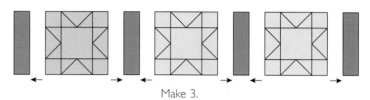

Make 3.

3. Lay out the units from Step 1 and the rows from Step 2, as shown in the assembly diagram. Sew the rows together. Press.

BORDERS

1. Join the 1½"-wide blue-and-white stripe strips end to end. Measure the quilt top through the center from top to bottom, then trim the inner border strips to this measurement. Sew the strips to the sides of the quilt. Press the seams toward the inner border strips.

2. Measure the quilt top through the center from side to side, including the inner border strips. Trim, sew, and press as in Step 1.

3. Sew the 6½"-wide multicolored fruit print outer border strips to the sides, top, and bottom of the quilt. Press the seams toward the outer border strips.

FINISHING

Follow the General Instructions (pages 11–12) to layer, baste, and quilt your quilt. Sew the 2⅛"-wide blue print strips together end to end with diagonal seams, and use them to bind the edges.

Alex's Tip   It's important to get a perspective on your work-in-progress to make appropriate decisions about the balance of color, shape, and value in the individual blocks and in the overall quilt design. I can't stress enough how valuable my design wall is to me when I am making my quilts.

My design wall is made from panels of Celotex (a type of wallboard available at hardware stores or home building centers) that I've covered with gridded flannel and attached to the wall. Other, more temporary options include a ¼"-thick panel of foamcore that you can store under the bed, or even the reverse side of a flannel-backed plastic tablecloth that you can tack to the wall.

A reducing glass gives you additional distance from (and perspective on) your design. Look for this handy tool at your local quilt shop or in catalogs or on websites that cater to quilters.

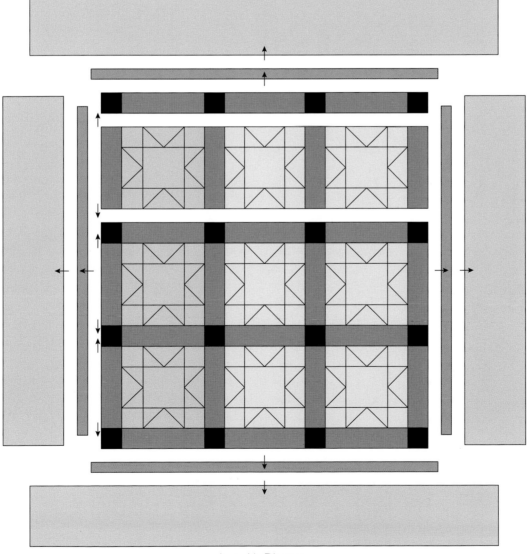

Assembly Diagram

About the Author

Alex Anderson's love affair with quiltmaking began in 1978, when she completed her *Grandmother's Flower Garden* quilt as part of her work toward a degree in art at San Francisco State University. Over the years, her focus has rested on understanding fabric relationships and on an intense appreciation for traditional quilting surface design and star quilts.

Alex currently hosts the popular Home and Garden Television and DIY Network quilt show *Simply Quilts* and is spokesperson for Bernina of America. Her quilts have appeared in numerous magazines, often in articles devoted specifically to her work.

Alex has two children and lives in Northern California with her husband, two cats, one dog, and the challenges of feeding various wildlife in her backyard. Visit her website at alexandersonquilts.com.

For more information,
ask for a free catalog:
C&T Publishing, Inc.
P.O. Box 1456
Lafayette, CA 94549
(800) 284-1114
Email:ctinfo@ctpub.com
Website: www.ctpub.com

For quilting supplies:
Cotton Patch Mail Order
3405 Hall Lane, Dept. CTB
Lafayette, CA 94549
(800) 835-4418
(925) 283-7883
Email: quiltusa@yahoo.com
Website: www.quiltusa.com

Other Books
by Alex Anderson